JAPANESE MYTHOLOGY

Tengu

BY JEAN KUO LEE

CONTENT CONSULTANT
HARUKO WAKABAYASHI, PhD
ASSOCIATE TEACHING PROFESSOR OF ASIAN LANGUAGES
AND CULTURES
RUTGERS UNIVERSITY

Kids Core
An Imprint of Abdo Publishing
abdobooks.com

abdobooks.com

Published by Abdo Publishing, a division of ABDO, PO Box 398166, Minneapolis, Minnesota 55439.

Printed in the United States of America, North Mankato, Minnesota.
102024
012025

Cover Photos: Shutterstock Images (foreground, background)
Interior Photos: Deborah Van Kirk/Alamy, 4–5, 28 (bottom); Brian Greenhow/Shutterstock Images, 6; Sean Pavone/Shutterstock Images, 8; John Stevenson/Asian Art & Archaeology, Inc./Corbis Historical/Getty Images, 10–11, 28 (top); Shutterstock Images, 13, 14, 24, 29 (top), 29 (bottom); John Navajo/Shutterstock Images, 15; Red Line Editorial, 16; Heritage Art/Heritage Images/Hulton Archive/Getty Images, 18, 20–21; Kelly Cheng/Moment Unreleased/Getty Images, 23; Daniel Mejia Novoa/Shutterstock Images, 26

Editor: Christa Kelly
Series Designer: Ryan Gale

Library of Congress Control Number: 2024938399

Publisher's Cataloging-in-Publication Data

Names: Lee, Jean Kuo, author.
Title: Tengu / by Jean Kuo Lee
Description: Minneapolis, Minnesota: ABDO Publishing, 2025 | Series: Japanese mythology | Includes online resources and index.
Identifiers: ISBN 9781098295998 (lib. bdg.) | ISBN 9798384916994 (ebook)
Subjects: LCSH: Mythology, Japanese--Juvenile literature. | Deities--Juvenile literature. | Tengu (Japanese goblin)--Juvenile literature. | Fabled creatures--Juvenile literature. | Goblins--Juvenile literature. | Tricksters--Juvenile literature. | Mythology, Asian--Juvenile literature.
Classification: DDC 398.21--dc23

CONTENTS

Some tengu carry a magical feather fan.

CHAPTER 1

The Magic Cape

High in the mountains of Japan was a forest. The forest was said to be home to **mythical** creatures called *tengu*. Tengu looked like humans but were red with long noses. They played tricks on people.

Tengu are very proud. They think that they are better than humans.

Everyone knew to stay away from the tengu. Everyone except a **mischievous** young boy.

The boy was not afraid of tengu. He wanted to find them. He had heard stories about a tengu with a magic cape. Anyone who wore the cape became invisible. The tengu used it to cause mischief without being seen.

"I want that cape," said the boy. He set out into the mountains to find it. When he came upon the tengu and its magic cape, he thought of a plan. The boy reached for a hollow piece of bamboo and held it to his eye. He pretended it was magical. "I can see everything near and far!" the boy exclaimed.

When the tengu saw the boy, it wanted the bamboo. "I'll let you try my magic cape if you let me try your magic bamboo," the tengu said.

Shinto

Many people in Japan practice a religion called Shinto. The word *Shinto* means "way of the gods." Followers of Shinto worship *kami*, or "spirits." Many stories about mythical creatures come from Shinto **mythology**.

More than 123 million people live in Japan.

The boy agreed and they swapped objects. In an instant, the boy disappeared beneath the cape and ran away. By the time the tengu realized it had been tricked, the boy was gone.

Kami and *Yōkai*

Japan is a country in Asia. It is made up of islands. People in Japan have been telling stories for more than a thousand years. Many of these stories center around spirits. Good spirits that are worshipped are called *kami*. Spirits that are not worshipped are called *yōkai*. These spirits often become angry and evil.

Some tengu are worshipped as protectors of mountains. These tengu are kami. Other tengu are cruel. They want to hurt humans. These tengu are *yōkai*. For hundreds of years, these creatures have fascinated people around the world.

Explore Online

Visit the website below. Does it give new information about tengu that wasn't in Chapter One?

Tengu

abdocorelibrary.com/tengu

Tengu can make people see things that aren't there.

Spirits and Sword Fighters

There are many types of tengu. Some are mischievous creatures. These tengu tumble rocks down the mountainside. They can make wind and hail. They make voices and laughter come from nowhere. They may even kidnap people from the forest.

Some tengu are even scarier. They can control people's minds. They cause storms and make people ill. They can even cause wars.

Many tengu target people who practice Buddhism. Buddhism is a religion from India. Some Buddhist people become **monks**. Tengu try to make monks do bad things. If they succeed, the monks become tengu too. But often monks will see through the tengu's scheme. They then pray and **banish** the tengu.

The Many Shapes of Tengu

Throughout history, tengu have been described in many different ways. Some tengu look like humans but are red with long noses. These tengu are called *daitengu*.

Daitengu rule over the other tengu.

Kotengu are also known as *karasu*.

Other tengu look like a cross between a bird and a human. They have long beaks and wings. These tengu are called *kotengu*. *Kotengu* attack people with their sharp claws.

Tengu can also disguise themselves. Sometimes they look like normal birds. They often take the form of black kites. Black kites

The Japanese word for "black kite" is *tobi.*

are birds that look like hawks. Tengu can also disguise themselves as regular people. Sometimes they disguise themselves as monks. Other times they pretend to be holy people or pretty women. They use their disguises to trick people.

Mount Kurama is in southern Japan.

Mount Kurama

Mount Kurama is a deeply forested mountain near the city of Kyoto. The mountain is home to King Sōjōbō, the king of the tengu. King Sōjōbō looks human, with white hair and a red robe. Sometimes he is described as having a long nose. His tengu followers look part bird and part human.

King Sōjōbō is very powerful. He is an expert sword fighter. He is also good to humans. According to legend, he and his tengu followers took in a young boy named Ushiwakamaru. They trained Ushiwakamaru in martial arts.

Samurai

After Ushiwakamaru was trained by the tengu, he became a famous samurai. Samurai were expert warriors. They were particularly skilled at fighting with swords and bows. From 1192 to 1868, the samurai were among the most powerful groups in Japan.

Minamoto no Yoshitsune's training is detailed in the famous Japanese play *Kurama-tengu.*

They taught him sword fighting. The boy grew into a great warrior. He won many battles. He became known as Minamoto no Yoshitsune.

Primary Source

People describe tengu in many different ways. William Elliot Griffis provides one description:

> Curious creatures are the tengu, with the head of a hawk and the body of a man. They have very hairy hands or paws with two fingers, and feet with two toes. They are hatched out of eggs and have wings and feathers until they are full grown.

Source: William Elliot Griffis. *Japanese Fairy World: Stories from the Wonder-lore of Japan*. James H. Barhyte, 1880, p. 112.

Comparing Texts

Does this quote support the information in this chapter? Or does it give a different perspective? Explain how in a few sentences.

People have been telling stories about tengu for more than a thousand years. Tengu even appear in *The Tale of Genji*, the world's first novel.

CHAPTER 3

Tengu in Japanese Culture

No one is sure where the idea of tengu came from. Some think stories about tengu came from India or China. Others think myths about the creatures came from tribes in Central Asia. Still others think the creature was based on another monster called a griffin.

Tengu have become an important part of everyday life in Japan. People in Japan often describe others as tengu. A person who acts like a tengu is said to be arrogant or conceited. However, tengu can also represent a fierce, free, and wild spirit. In the past, stories about tengu inspired peasants to rebel. If they were facing harsh rulers, they could fight back like the tengu who do not follow human rules.

Honoring Tengu

Tengu are worshipped at several mountains, **shrines**, and Buddhist temples in Japan. Kuramadera Temple is one of the most important temples. It marks the home of King Sōjōbō.

Kuramadera Temple was founded in 770 CE.

The portable shrines used during festivals are called *mikoshi*.

Jirōbō is another important tengu. He is worshipped in the mountains of Hira. He and other tengu are also honored at Shinto shrines.

Tengu play an important role during festivals. The annual Matsuri festival honors kami.

Tengu are said to guard the portable shrines used during the celebration.

Tengu in Art

Tengu appear in many **traditional** Japanese woodblock prints. These prints are made by carving text and images into pieces of wood to make a stamp. The stamp is then covered in ink. Paper is placed onto the stamp to make a print.

Senjafuda

Senjafuda is a type of woodblock print. These prints are done on small slips of paper. Sometimes these prints have pictures of *yōkai* such as tengu. Some people leave these slips at shrines as offerings. Others collect them.

Japanese masks are traditionally made out of cypress wood.

Tengu masks are also popular. These masks are red with long noses or beaks. People wear them during Shinto festivals and parades. They are also often seen in Japanese plays.

The masks can even be used as decorations to frighten bad spirits.

Today, tengu appear in many Japanese cartoons. These are called anime. Tengu also appear in Japanese comic books, or manga. Popular video games such as *Pokémon* and *Mega Man* also include characters based on tengu. Throughout Japan and around the world, the tengu has become a widespread figure.

Further Evidence

Look at the website below. Does it give any new evidence to support Chapter Three?

Kuramadera

abdocorelibrary.com/tengu

Legendary Facts

Tengu are mythical creatures from Japan.

Some tengu are good. Others are mischievous or evil.

Some tengu have human bodies with long, red noses. Others have wings and beaks.

Today, tengu are found in art throughout Japan.

Glossary

banish
force to leave an area

mischievous
describing someone who causes trouble

monks
people who have taken religious vows and devote their lives to prayer

mythical
appearing in myths

mythology
stories about a specific group's gods and religious figures

shrines
places where gods and other religious figures are honored and worshipped

traditional
relating to practices from the past

Online Resources

To learn more about tengu and Japanese mythology, visit our free resource websites below.

Visit **abdocorelibrary.com** or scan this QR code for free Common Core resources for teachers and students, including vetted activities, multimedia, and booklinks, for deeper subject comprehension.

Visit **abdobooklinks.com** or scan this QR code for free additional online weblinks for further learning. These links are routinely monitored and updated to provide the most current information available.

Learn More

Andrews, Elizabeth. *Buddhism*. Abdo, 2024.

Kaiser, Emma. *Kitsune*. Abdo, 2025.

Krensky, Stephen. *The Book of Mythical Beasts & Magical Creatures*. DK, 2020.

Index

About the Author

Jean Kuo Lee is an Asian American author who lives in California. She loves seeing tengu characters in films and games.